BATTLEFIELDS ACROSS AMERICA

SHILOH

RICHARD STEINS

Twenty-First Century Books

A Division of Henry Holt and Company

New York

Twenty-First Century Books
A Division of Henry Holt and Company, Inc.
115 West 18th Street
New York, New York 10011

Henry Holt® and colophon are registered trademarks of Henry Holt and
Company, Inc.
Publishers since 1866

Published in Canada by Fitzhenry & Whiteside Ltd.
195 Allstate Parkway, Markham, Ontario L3R 4T8

Printed in the United States of America on acid free paper ∞.

Created and produced in association with Blackbirch Graphics, Inc.

Picture Credits
Cover and page 51: David A. Harvey/©National Geographic Society; pages 4, 6,
9, 11, 16, 18, 19, 20, 21, 23, 24-25, 30, 35-36, 39, 40, 46: ©North Wind Picture
Archives; page 12: Library of Congress; page 14: Unident Photographers/NPG;
page 29: Matthew Brady/NPG; page 31: J. McRae/ NPG; pages 48, 50: ©Bruce
Dale/ National Geographic Society; page 55: ©James P. Bagsby/ Fort Donelson
National Battlefield; page 57: Courtesy of National Park Service, Manhattan Sites.
All maps by Bob Italiano/©Blackbirch Graphics, Inc.

Library of Congress Cataloging-in-Publication Data

Steins, Richard.
    Shiloh / Richard Steins.
        p.   cm. — (Battlefields Across America)
    Includes bibliographical references and index.
    ISBN 0-8050-5229-1
    1. Shiloh, Battle of, 1862—Juvenile literature. 2. Shiloh National Military
Park (Tenn.)—Juvenile literature. I. Title. II. Series.
E473.54.S74   1997
973.7'31—dc21   97-17229
                                                                     CIP
                                                                      AC

CONTENTS

P A R T   O N E

AMERICANS AGAINST AMERICANS:
THE CIVIL WAR

The Constitution of the United States, which established America's democratic form of government, went into effect in March 1789. In its Preamble—the opening statement—the writers of the Constitution stated that the new government was created in order to "form a more perfect Union," and to "insure domestic Tranquillity...."

In the late 1780s, the leaders of the new nation believed that the best way to maintain peace was to ignore a highly controversial issue—slavery. In 1789, there were about 3,900,000 people living in the United States. Approximately 760,000 (or one in five people) were African-American slaves.

Some people wanted to get rid of slavery by abolishing it entirely. Others passionately defended it. The framers of the Constitution realized that because Americans felt so strongly about this issue, it had the potential to split the new country apart. Rather than addressing slavery directly, the writers of the Constitution chose to create the "three-fifths compromise." Slavery was not mentioned specifically, but for purposes of counting the population of each state—and therefore determining representation in Congress—every five slaves would be counted as only three free people. The Constitution does not even use the word slavery. Instead, in Article I, Section 2, slaves are referred to as "all other persons."

"A Common Bond of Principle"

The issue of slavery, however, did not go away. Many of the new nation's leaders understood the danger it posed to the unity of the United States. Although he owned slaves, President George Washington wrote, "I can clearly foresee that nothing but the rooting out of slavery

< 5 >

In the South, slaves were often used to do the difficult work of picking and processing cotton.

can perpetuate the existence of our union, by considering it in a common bond of principle."[1]

That common bond, however, was not forged in the early years of the nation. In 1789, although slavery still existed in the North, it was rapidly disappearing from that region. By 1804, the Northern states had abolished slavery by passing laws that made it illegal. In addition, the economy in the North was based on small farms and

< 7 >

businesses and other kinds of work for which slave labor was not particularly useful.

In the South, however, things were very different. Slavery was an important part of the region's largely agricultural economy. From as far north as Virginia and the Chesapeake region, and south to the interior of Mississippi, most farming—especially the growing of cotton, sugar, and rice—relied on some form of slave labor. In the deep South, for example, large cotton plantations used hundreds of slaves to hand pick the cotton in the fields.

Even small farmers in parts of the upper South such as Kentucky and Tennessee often owned slaves. Although slavery had disappeared in the North, it continued in the South—and even grew. White Southerners felt strongly that they should not be forced to give up their right to own slaves.

The Missouri Compromise

Why was slavery such a divisive issue between the North and the South? The main reason was political power. In Congress, the rivalry between the North and the South centered around the question of slavery. Southerners believed that if slavery was either limited or abolished, their economy would suffer along with their way of life. The North, with its free states (where slavery was illegal) and business economy, would then have more power over the South. To prevent this from happening, the Southern states fiercely opposed any attempts to limit slavery.

In addition, Southerners lived in constant fear of slave rebellion. In some counties, slaves actually formed a majority of the population. Most white Southerners were afraid that if slaves had any form of freedom, they would rise up and kill their masters. Even though there had been few slave rebellions in the South since

< 8 >

the introduction of slavery in the early 1600s, whites still feared that there would be rebellion if slavery was tampered with in any way.

In 1808, Congress banned the importation of slaves from abroad. The slave population of the United States continued to expand, however, as slaves had children who were also put to work. To help keep slavery alive, Southerners wanted the territories in the West to allow slavery. Northerners, on the other hand, feared the growth of "slave power" and generally opposed the westward expansion of slavery.

In 1820, the Missouri territory applied for admission to the Union as a slave state. At that time, there were 11 free states and 11 slave states. The admission of another slave state would tip the balance of power toward the South. The opportunity for compromise came when Maine applied for admission as a free state. The Missouri Compromise of 1820 preserved the balance of power between the North and the South with 12 free and 12 slave states. In addition, the agreement prohibited the expansion of slavery into the northern part of the Louisiana Purchase territory. This compromise allowed the expansion of slavery into the southern and western portions of the country, but restricted slavery from moving northward into the territories.

The Kansas-Nebraska Act

The Missouri Compromise temporarily resolved the dispute over the future of slavery in the United States. But the controversy was reignited in 1854, when Congress created the Kansas-Nebraska Territories. The Kansas-Nebraska Act called for the exercise of "popular sovereignty" in the new territories. Under this provision, slavery was not specifically prohibited or approved. Instead, the settlers were the given the power to decide if their state would be

< 9 >

admitted to the Union as a slave or free state.

The Kansas-Nebraska Act was sponsored by a prominent Democrat, Senator Stephen A. Douglas of Illinois. The new act, in effect, repealed the Missouri Compromise, allowing the people living in any of the territories to decide whether or not to be a slave state by voting on the issue.

The Kansas-Nebraska Act led to violence in Kansas. Fighting broke out between proslavery and antislavery settlers, who burned each other's

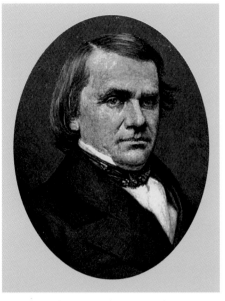

Senator Stephen A. Douglas sponsored the Kansas-Nebraska Act.

settlements. Over the next few years, hostility between Americans who favored slavery and those who opposed it increased throughout the nation. Each side grew ever more fearful that the other side would gain the upper hand in government. The Southerners felt certain that an increase in the number of free states would lead to the abolition of slavery. The Northerners feared a nation in which the evil of slavery would be allowed to expand as far as the West Coast under the protection of the doctrine of popular sovereignty.

An Angry Man from Illinois

The passage of the Kansas-Nebraska Act enraged one Illinois citizen in particular—Abraham Lincoln, a well-known lawyer from Springfield. He had been involved briefly in state politics and served one term in the U.S. Congress in the 1840s as a member of the Whig

< 10 >

party. Lincoln had then returned to Illinois to work as a lawyer and to raise his young family.

Lincoln detested slavery. Even though he believed that the federal government did not have the right to outlaw the institution, he thought that it should be prohibited from expanding. Lincoln felt that if slavery were not allowed to expand, it would slowly disappear from the South.

Angry at the passage of the 1854 law and the reversal of the Missouri Compromise, Lincoln vowed to return to politics to fight against popular sovereignty. He ran unsuccessfully for the U.S. Senate in 1854, but he was undeterred by this loss and continued to work as a member of the newly founded Republican party. The Republican party was formed to oppose the expansion of slavery, and Lincoln soon became known as one of the party's most eloquent spokesmen.

Lincoln ran for the Senate again in 1858, this time against Senator Douglas. During the campaign, Lincoln and Douglas staged a series of famous debates on slavery, which were held throughout the state of Illinois. In one debate, Lincoln attacked the idea that popular sovereignty would solve the dispute between the North and the South. He said,

*Under the operation of that policy, that agitation has not only not **ceased**, but has **constantly augmented**. In **my** opinion, it **will** not cease, until a **crisis** shall have been reached, and passed. 'A House divided against itself cannot stand.' I believe this government cannot endure, permanently half **slave** and half **free**.*[2]

Although Lincoln lost the election, he became the Republican party's most prominent figure and a leading presidential candidate in 1860.

On October 7, 1858, Douglas and Lincoln met at Knox College in Galesburg, Illinois, for their fifth debate on slavery.

< 12 >

The Election of 1860

Tension over the issue of slavery reached its peak between 1859 and 1860. In 1859, John Brown, a Northerner and a strong opponent of slavery, attempted to start a slave rebellion at Harpers Ferry, Virginia. Although the uprising was quickly crushed by federal troops and Brown was hanged by the state of Virginia, white Southerners became more convinced than ever that Northerners were actively trying to destroy their way of life.

John Brown opposed slavery and tried to start a slave rebellion in 1859.

In 1860, members of the Democratic party were split over the issue of slavery. When Senator Douglas, a Northerner, was nominated to run for president of the United States, Southern Democrats left the party and nominated their own candidate for president— Vice President John C. Breckinridge. With the Democrats divided politically, and with yet

< 13 >

another candidate in the race (John C. Bell of the Constitutional Union party), the Republican party was favored to win.

In June 1860, the Republicans nominated Abraham Lincoln as their candidate for president. In the months before the election, Lincoln repeatedly stated that despite his opposition to the expansion of slavery, he would not try to abolish it if elected president.

The South, however, did not believe Lincoln. Most Southern leaders were convinced that his election would be a major threat to their "peculiar institution," as they referred to slavery. When Lincoln won in November 1860, the stage was set for drastic action.

Secession

Some Southern political leaders thought that passions needed time to cool. Others, however, were more excited than ever and demanded that the South secede—withdraw from the Union.

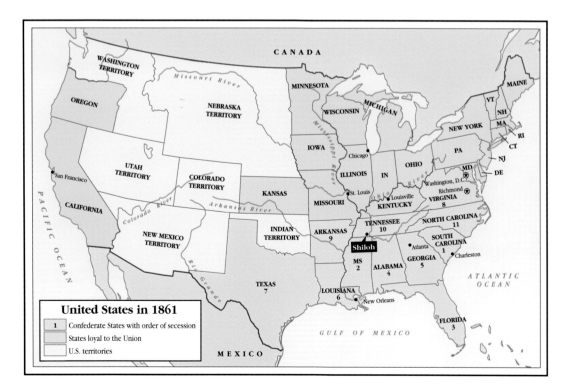

United States in 1861

1	Confederate States with order of secession
	States loyal to the Union
	U.S. territories

< 14 >

Jefferson Davis became the first president of the Confederacy in 1861.

One, by one, the states of the South began to secede. South Carolina was the first to do so in December 1860. It was soon followed by Mississippi, Florida, Alabama, Georgia, Louisiana, and Texas. These states had all seceded by the time Lincoln was inaugurated as president on March 4, 1861. In February 1861, Southern leaders had met in Montgomery, Alabama, and formed the Confederate States of America. The new Confederacy selected Jefferson Davis of Mississippi, a former U.S. Senator and secretary of war, as its first president.

The War Begins

Lincoln's position on secession was clear: It was illegal. The Constitution, he believed, had created an indivisible nation that could not be split by an act of secession. But how was he to prevent this and make the seven rebellious states return to the Union?

During the early weeks of his presidency, Lincoln pondered this dilemma but he could find no easy solution. In the end, the question was resolved for him by the Confederacy. In April 1861, Lincoln attempted to send provisions to Fort Sumter, a Union military fort on an island in the harbor of Charleston, South Carolina. In response, Confederate forces bombarded and captured the fort. Shortly after, four more states—Virginia, Arkansas, Tennessee, and

< 15 >

North Carolina—seceded from the Union. The United States had been divided.

In his inaugural address in March, Lincoln had said, "In *your* hands, my dissatisfied fellow countrymen, and not in *mine*, is the momentous issue of civil war." He appealed to all Americans to remember their common heritage and continued:

> *The mystic chords of memory, stretching from every battle-field, and patriot grave, to every living heart and hearthstone, all over this broad land, will yet swell the chorus of the Union, when again touched, as surely they will be, by the better angels of our nature.*[3]

But by April, the dissatisfied Southerners had spoken. It was to be war.

P A R T   T W O

SHILOH: THE BATTLE FOR THE WEST

With the attack on Fort Sumter, Lincoln realized that for the Union to be reunited, the Confederacy would have to be defeated in war. But what should the North's military strategy be? The country had fought the British during the American Revolution and again during the War of 1812. But Americans had never before fought fellow Americans.

In 1861, the 22 Northern states had a population of about 22 million people. The 11 Southern states had a population of about 9.5 million, of whom 3.5 million were slaves. The North was the industrial part of the country—it had the capability to produce weapons and military equipment and had most of the nation's railroads. In contrast, the South was mainly agricultural—it did not have much industry and had few rail lines. In addition, more than one third of its population—the slaves—could not serve the Confederacy as soldiers because the Confederate government would not allow them to take up arms.

Strategies for Victory

The Confederacy occupied a vast territory that was difficult to defend from outside attack. There were no real natural boundaries—such as high mountains or deep rivers—that could protect the thousands of miles along its border with the North.

Most Southern strategists believed that the Confederate States of America would need to win the war quickly, by a dramatic defeat that would shatter the morale of the North—for example, capturing the Union capital of Washington, D.C. Southern military and political lead-ers hoped that the swift capture of Washington, D.C.—which was

< 17 >

Textile companies were just one of the industries that gave the Union an advantage in the Civil War.

< 19 >

directly across the Potomac River from Confederate Virginia—would so shock the North that it would be willing to end the war and allow the Confederacy its independence as a separate country.

Lincoln and his advisers developed their own military plans. Their strategy had three main objectives: (1) target Southern armies and demoralize the South; (2) blockade the Confederacy by sea, consequently preventing it from trading with foreign countries—especially Great Britain; and (3) in the West, gain control of the Mississippi River and the city of New Orleans which would divide the Confederacy down the middle.

New Orleans was a bustling port city at the start of the Civil War.

< 20 >

Armies in the West

The Union plan to gain control of the Mississippi River was put into operation with various military actions in the West in early 1862. The Confederate leaders had several hundred miles of territory to defend, from the Mississippi River through Kentucky and Tennessee, and as far east as Virginia.

Confederate Forces

In February 1862, the Confederate forces in Kentucky and northern Tennessee were led by General Albert Sidney Johnston. The 70,000 men under his command were scattered in irregular formations along a 500-mile line. Their assignment was to defend the region against, and repel, any invading force from the north.

Major-General Leonidas Polk of the Confederacy

Johnston's army was divided into three main groups. The largest group, of about 25,000 men, was centered in Bowling Green, Kentucky. Further west, another 17,000 men under the command of Major-General Leonidas Polk were located in Columbus, Kentucky. Stationed between Johnston and Polk was the smallest group of men— about 5,000. They were assigned to defend two important fortifications in northern Tennessee— Fort Henry and Fort Donelson.

These two forts were 12 miles apart and were situated

< 21 >

directly between the Tennessee and Cumberland rivers. Together, the two forts served as the Confederates' main defense against an invading force sailing down the two rivers from Kentucky in the north.

Union Forces

There were also about 125,000 Union soldiers in the West. They were scattered in three large groups: the Army of the Ohio, a 55,000-man force under Brigadier-General Don Carlos Buell stationed in Louisville, Kentucky; a 20,000-

Brigadier-General Don Carlos Buell of the Union

man unit based in Cairo, Illinois, and commanded by Brigadier-General Ulysses S. Grant; and Brigadier-General John Pope's army of about 30,000 soldiers based in the state of Missouri.

The Union forces had an important weapon, which the Confederates lacked—gunboats specially designed to operate in the shallow rivers of the West. These gunboats were based in Cairo, where they could operate with Grant's forces. The boats would play a vital role in the Union's battle for the West.

The Capture of Forts Henry and Donelson

The goal of the Union forces was to drive the Confederate armies out of Kentucky and Tennessee and thereby weaken Confederate control of this region near the Mississippi River. Johnston knew that he had fewer men than were in the Union forces. He realized that

Albert Sidney Johnston was born in Washington, Kentucky, in 1803. As a young man, he enlisted in the U.S. Army and fought against the Indians in the Black Hawk War (1832) in Illinois.

The young officer wanted more excitement, however, and so in 1834, he quit the army and went to Texas—which was then part of Mexico. Johnston joined the revolutionary forces fighting for an independent Texas and soon became their commander. After Texas declared its independence, Johnston became the new republic's secretary of war (1838–1840).

Most Southerners who lived in Texas, however, were not interested in independence. They wanted to become part of the United States. When Texas accepted entry into the Union in 1845, war broke out between the United States and Mexico.

Once again, Johnston found himself fighting the Mexicans as head of a unit of volunteers, this time near the city of Monterrey, Mexico. In 1849, Johnston rejoined the U.S. Army.

During the 1850s, he served in a variety of posts in the West. By the time the Civil War broke out in 1861, Johnston was commander of the U.S. Army's Department of the Pacific. At the start of the war, he was offered a command in the Union army. Like many Southerners, however, Johnston decided to remain loyal to his adopted state. He resigned his commission and returned to his home in Austin, Texas. Shortly thereafter, he was appointed to a position in the newly

the Confederates would be defeated if the Union armies attacked them with full force.

The Southerners were spared that fate in the early months of 1862, because the two Union generals, Buell and Pope, were hesitant to attack. Buell was a courageous commander, but he preferred to act slowly and with caution. Instead of attacking the Confederate

formed Confederate army by President Jefferson Davis. In 1861, Davis made Johnston the commander of all Confederate forces in the West.

Johnston was over six feet tall and had an imposing physical presence. Like his chief opponent at Shiloh— Grant—Johnston was daring, brave, and not afraid to fight. However, the losses his army suffered at Forts Henry and Donelson were so upsetting to him that he gambled everything in the battle at Shiloh. Confederate President Davis considered him an indispensable soldier and was devastated when he heard the news of Johnston's death. Had Johnston survived, he might have become one of the great Southern commanders.

Albert Sidney Johnston was commander of all Confederate forces in the West.

forces near Bowling Green, he advanced carefully toward the city of Nashville, Tennessee. Buell did not want to risk a direct encounter with the Southerners.

In Missouri, Pope also decided against attacking the Confederates. Like Buell, he was reluctant to mount a full-scale assault. Because of the inaction of these two Union leaders, it was left up to

This illustration shows the hand-to-hand combat at Fort Donelson the day before the Confederates surrendered that fort.

Grant to make a decisive move. Unlike Buell and Pope, Grant was a ferocious fighter. He soon came up with a plan to attack Fort Henry. This was followed by a decision to attack Fort Donelson.

Fort Henry fell swiftly to a Union gunboat attack on February 6, 1862. Harsh weather delayed Grant's march on Fort Donelson for several days. When the weather briefly improved, however, Grant and his army aggressively attacked the fort. The Confederates surrendered Fort Donelson on February 16, 1862.

When the Confederate commander of the fort, Brigadier-General Simon B. Buckner, asked Grant for surrender terms, Grant replied,

"No terms except an unconditional and immediate surrender can be accepted. I propose to move immediately upon your works."[1] Thus, he earned his nickname, "Unconditional Surrender" Grant, which coincidentally matched his first two initials (U.S.).

Grant's Union forces suffered 3,000 dead and wounded in the fight for Forts Henry and Donelson, while the Confederates counted 2,000 dead and wounded. The Confederates also lost about 13,000 men who were taken prisoner. Most of these soldiers were reinforcements sent by Johnston to help defend the forts. The Union victories were the result of Grant's willingness to fight—and to fight hard.

< 26 >

The Road to Shiloh

With the loss of so many men, Johnston realized that his situation in Tennessee was desperate. Appealing to President Jefferson Davis for reinforcements, Johnston ordered his forces to retreat.

The Confederates moved south, across the Tennessee border, to a spot near the town of Corinth, Mississippi. Corinth was located near the Memphis and Charleston Railroad, the only railroad line in the South linking the Mississippi River and the Atlantic coast. At Corinth, Johnston gathered reinforcements, and his army grew to about 56,000 men.

The Confederates Regroup

The army was reorganized and divided into four corps. General P. G. T. Beauregard, who had ordered the attack on Fort Sumter and had recently arrived from the east, was named second-in-command after Johnston. Although morale among the troops was high, they faced serious problems. Poor sanitary conditions and improper preparation of food were common and led to much illness. The troops were weak and were susceptible to infectious diseases such as pneumonia, measles, typhoid fever, and chicken pox. Of the 56,000 Confederate soldiers under Johnston, only 44,000 men were well enough to fight.

The Confederates also suffered from a shortage of weapons and ammunition. Johnston had ordered more than 18,000 new rifles, but most of them had not been delivered. The soldiers were forced to use older guns.

Johnston was well aware of these drawbacks. He was disappointed by the losses of Forts Henry and Donelson, however, and wanted to defeat the Union. The Confederate commander was determined to pounce on the Union army at the first opportunity.

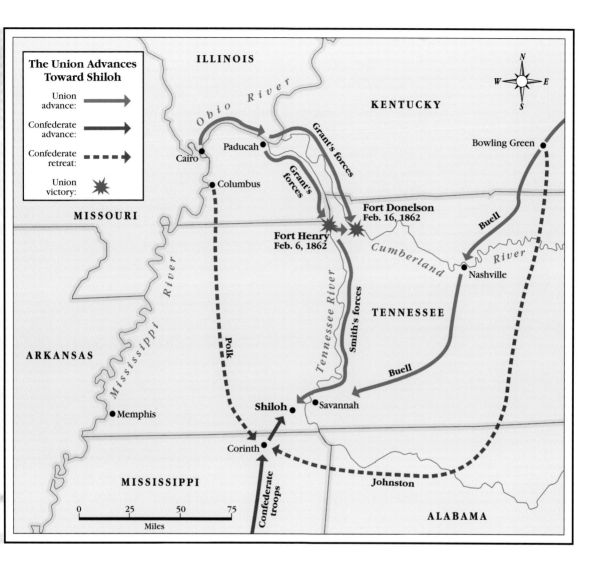

The Union Advances Toward Shiloh

Union advance:

Confederate advance:

Confederate retreat:

Union victory:

ILLINOIS

Ohio River

KENTUCKY

Cairo

Paducah

Bowling Green

Columbus

Grant's forces

Grant's forces

Buell

MISSOURI

Fort Donelson
Feb. 16, 1862

Fort Henry
Feb. 6, 1862

Cumberland River

Nashville

Smith's forces

Tennessee River

TENNESSEE

ARKANSAS

Mississippi River

Polk

Buell

Memphis

Shiloh

Savannah

Corinth

MISSISSIPPI

Confederate troops

Johnston

0   25   50   75
Miles

ALABAMA

Union Blunders

By early April 1862, the Confederates' chances had improved because of a series of mistakes made by the Union forces. Perhaps the greatest piece of luck to come the Confederates' way was the removal of Grant from his command immediately after his victories at Forts Henry and Donelson. Grant's superior, Major-General Henry Halleck, thought Grant was a brave, but reckless fighter and wanted

Ulysses S. Grant was born in Point Pleasant, Ohio, in 1822. His birth name was Hiram Ulysses Grant. As a youth, he worked in his family's farming business. Later, he received an appointment to the U.S. Military Academy at West Point, and graduated in 1843. Upon enrollment, he was incorrectly listed as "Ulysses S. Grant," and he retained that name for the rest of his life.

Based on the events of his early life, no one could have predicted that Grant would become one of the greatest American generals in history. At West Point, he was an average student, although he excelled in horsemanship. He served with distinction in the Mexican War in the 1840s, then received a series of appointments to insignificant posts in the West.

His western assignments led to long separations from his beloved wife Julia and their children. During these times, Grant was depressed and often drank heavily. His drinking finally got him into trouble, and he was forced to resign from the army in 1854.

As a civilian, Grant tried farming and a variety of busines ventures, but all his attempts to make money failed. Finally, he was offered a job as a clerk in a leather-goods store owned by members of his family in Galena, Illinois. It seemed that Grant would remain there for the rest of his life, an unknown clerk and a failed army officer.

Then came the Civil War. Grant volunteered his services to the state of Illinois and was soon appointed a colonel of the 21st Illinois Volunteers by the governor. Grant proved a highly popular commander as well as a brilliant organizer and strategist. In 1861, he was made a brigadier-general. Early in 1862, Grant fought his winning battles at Forts Henry and Donelson before moving on to Shiloh.

After the battle of Shiloh, Grant rose quickly in the army. He had the primary quality that President Abraham Lincoln was looking for in a commander: the willingness to fight hard. At a time when many army generals were fearful of taking risks in battle, Grant never hesitated to plunge his army into the midst of conflict. Grant was so aggressive that he was often labeled a "butcher" because of the large numbers of casualties he was willing to sustain. Shiloh, Grant later recorded, taught him that the war would last a long time. "Up until the battle of Shiloh, I, as well as thousands of other citizens, believed that the rebellion against the Government would collapse suddenly and soon if a decided victory could be gained over any of its armies . . . ." After Shiloh, he "gave up all idea of saving the Union except by complete conquest."[2]

Unlike Johnston, Grant was undistinguished in appearance. He was relatively short and uninterested in displaying his rank. Instead of elaborate uniforms, he usually wore the plain shirt of an ordinary private and simple trousers.

Grant rose in rank to become commander of all Union forces in 1864. The following year he accepted the surrender of General Robert E. Lee at Appomattox, Virginia. After the war, Grant remained the head of the army. He was so popular among the people, however, that many hoped he would enter politics.

In 1868, Grant was nominated by the Republican party to run for the U.S. presidency. He was easily elected, becoming the 18th president on March 4, 1869, at the age of 46. As president, however, Grant was not a success. The brilliance and daring he showed on the battlefield were missing from his political career. His administration was riddled with corruption, and many people he considered friends betrayed his trust. Grant, however, was an honest man and was easily reelected in 1872.

After two terms, Grant left office on March 4, 1877, and moved to New York City. There, he invested his money with someone he trusted, who turned out to be dishonest. In his early 60s, the once great army general and former U.S. president had no money and few prospects. At this time, he was stricken with throat cancer. In order to provide for his family after his death, Grant began writing his memoirs. He finished them just a few days before he died in 1885 at the age of 63. The book sold quickly and earned a significant amount of money for his widow and children.

Grant is buried in a huge mausoleum on the Hudson River in New York City. Popularly called "Grant's Tomb," its official name is the General Grant National Memorial.

This photograph of Grant was taken by the famous Civil War photographer Matthew Brady.

< 30 >

to remove him from his post, despite his successes in battle. Halleck and his supporters accused Grant of incompetence and drunkenness.

Grant was replaced by Brigadier-General C. F. Smith. Halleck ordered Buell's forces to join Smith's. Although the Union armies concentrated their forces, they did not attack.

Arrival at Pittsburg Landing

Halleck sent Smith to sever the Memphis and Charleston Railroad. Needing to camp, one of Smith's officers, Brigadier-General William Tecumseh Sherman, came upon a favorable site called Pittsburg Landing.

This illustration of Pittsburg Landing, shown from the ferry dock on the opposite shore, was done from a photograph.

UNION COMMANDER: WILLIAM TECUMSEH SHERMAN

The Union general who was second only to Grant in fame and popularity was William Tecumseh Sherman. Born in Lancaster, Ohio, in 1820, he graduated from the military academy at West Point in 1840, and served in a variety of army posts in the South. Sherman served in the Mexican War and retired from the army in 1853 to become a banker and a lawyer. In the late 1850s, he accepted an appointment as superintendent of the state military academy in Louisiana. When Louisiana seceded from the Union, Sherman resigned and rejoined the Union army as a colonel.

William Tecumseh Sherman

Sherman was a genius at organization, as well as an aggressive fighter. Grant recognized these qualities and so ensured Sherman's promotion. Sherman's most noted military achievement was the capture of Atlanta, Georgia, and his "March to the Sea" that began in late 1864 and ended in the Carolinas in 1865.

Military historians consider Sherman one of the architects of modern warfare. Previously, military conflicts rarely involved civilians. Sherman brought warfare to the entire population of the South. On his "March to the Sea," his army burned and destroyed everything in sight, including civilian homes, barns, businesses, and railroads. His troops confiscated private property, freed slaves, and took chickens, pigs, and crops for food. Sherman believed that the people of the South should feel the sting of war personally. "I can make this march, and make Georgia howl!" Sherman assured Grant. "We have on hand over eight thousand head of cattle and three million rations of bread.... We can find plenty of forage [provisions] in the interior of the State."[3]

After the war, Sherman resisted all efforts to draw him into politics. In 1884, he refused to be considered for the Republican presidential nomination, saying, "If nominated I will not accept; if elected I will not serve!"[4]

Sherman commanded the army from 1869 (succeeding Grant) until 1884, at which time he retired. He died in 1891 at the age of 71.

< 32 >

It was located on the west bank of the river about 22 miles northeast of Corinth, to which it was connected by several country roads.

Smith's troops moved into the area around Pittsburg Landing. They established their camp on the wooded plateau between the river and a small, log meeting house called Shiloh Church, two miles southwest of Pittsburg Landing.

Shortly after his men arrived at Pittsburg Landing, Smith accidentally cut his leg. The wound became infected and he was unable to function effectively. Halleck was faced with a dilemma. He needed a quick replacement, and the only available—and qualified—person was Grant. Halleck restored Grant to his former command.

All the Union officers, including Grant, believed that the Confederates were too weak and demoralized to attack. Instead of having their men dig trenches and other fortifications, the camp was setup without a formal defensive arrangement. Although this made them highly vulnerable to attack, they did not believe that such an attack would come. Halleck's plan was for Grant to await Buell's arrival before attacking Johnston's forces at Corinth. This was a serious misjudgment. The cost for Halleck's error would be high.

The Battle: Day One, April 6, 1862

While the Union forces relaxed to the north, Johnston made his move. It was essential, he believed, to attack Grant's forces *before* Buell arrived. Beauregard, however, believed that the element of surprise would be lost because the Union would see and hear them coming. But Johnston disagreed. "I would fight them if they were a million," Johnston said.[5]

Twenty-two miles away, Grant's forces enjoyed the balmy spring morning. It was Sunday. The Union army's five divisions were spread out over the area near Pittsburg Landing. Some soldiers

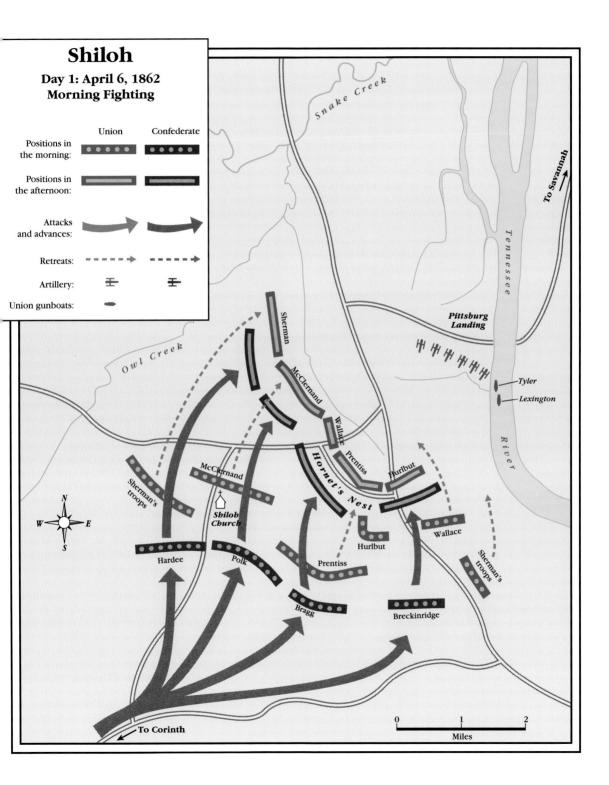

Shiloh
Day 1: April 6, 1862
Morning Fighting

	Union	Confederate
Positions in the morning:		
Positions in the afternoon:		
Attacks and advances:		
Retreats:		
Artillery:		
Union gunboats:		

Snake Creek

To Savannah

Pittsburg Landing

Tennessee River

Tyler

Lexington

Owl Creek

Sherman

McClernand

Wallace

Prentiss

Hornet's Nest

Hurlbut

Sherman's troops

McClernand

Shiloh Church

Prentiss

Hurlbut

Wallace

Sherman's troops

N W E S

Hardee

Polk

Bragg

Breckinridge

To Corinth

0	1	2

Miles

< 34 >

ate a leisurely breakfast and drank coffee, while others polished their rifles and boots or napped under the peach trees. On the river, a musician on one of the Union gunboats played songs. Private Leander Stilwell of the 61st Illinois Regiment remembered: "It really seemed like Sunday in the country at home. The boys were scattered around [camp]...polishing and brightening their muskets and brushing up and cleaning their shoes, jackets, [and] trousers."[6]

Confederates Attack

Nearby, 44,000 Confederate troops quietly sneaked into position. They were spread out in four parallel lines 1.5 miles wide. The central strategy of Johnston's plan was surprise: Attack the unsuspecting Union soldiers, cut off a retreat to the river, and force them to surrender quickly before they could regroup.

At 5:00 A.M. the battle began. Amidst the tremendous noise of rifle and artillery fire, and thousands of Confederate voices whooping out the "Rebel yell" (Confederate soldiers shouting in unison to frighten the enemy), the Confederate soldiers completely surprised the unsuspecting Union soldiers.

General Sherman, on a hill near the Shiloh Church, heard the racket and stepped out of his tent to see some 400 Confederate soldiers rushing toward him. Sherman's soldiers endured heavy fighting from 7:30 A.M. to 10:00 A.M. before retreating. The Southerners had finally overwhelmed Sherman's position. General Beauregard then moved his belongings into Sherman's recently evacuated tent.

Throughout the Union camps, panicky soldiers fled from the battlefield. By the end of the day, 5,000 men had run the two miles to the river, where they huddled beneath the bluffs. When the Confederate attack had begun, Grant was eight miles away, at Savannah, Tennessee. Hearing the cannon fire, he rushed by steamboat to Pittsburg Landing with reinforcements.

This illustration, drawn from a battlefield sketch, shows the Confederates capturing Union positions at Pittsburg Landing.

The Peach Orchard and the Hornet's Nest

By noon, Johnston believed that he had won the battle, relaying to Beauregard, "I think we shall press them to the river."[7] The Union line was still holding, however, especially at its center. There, troops fell back to a sunken road lined with trees. Troops in a separate position to the left were in a peach orchard. From protected positions along the road and in the orchard, Union troops fired at the advancing Confederates and managed to hold them back. At one point, the gunfire from the peach orchard was so intense that the

< 36 >

pink peach blossom petals falling from the trees formed a delicate blanket on the dead and wounded soldiers.

The Confederates made a total of 12 assaults on the Union lines on the road and in the orchard. So severe was the fighting there that the Confederates named the area the "Hornet's Nest." Johnston, riding his horse Fire-Eater, personally directed a charge toward the peach orchard. Bullets flew all around the Confederate commander, tearing his uniform and nicking his boots.

Several minutes later, Johnston realized that he had been shot in the leg. The wound did not seem serious at first, and Johnston was too absorbed in the battle to pay much attention to his injury.

Bullets flew in all directions in the "Hornet's Nest," where some of the heaviest fighting took place.

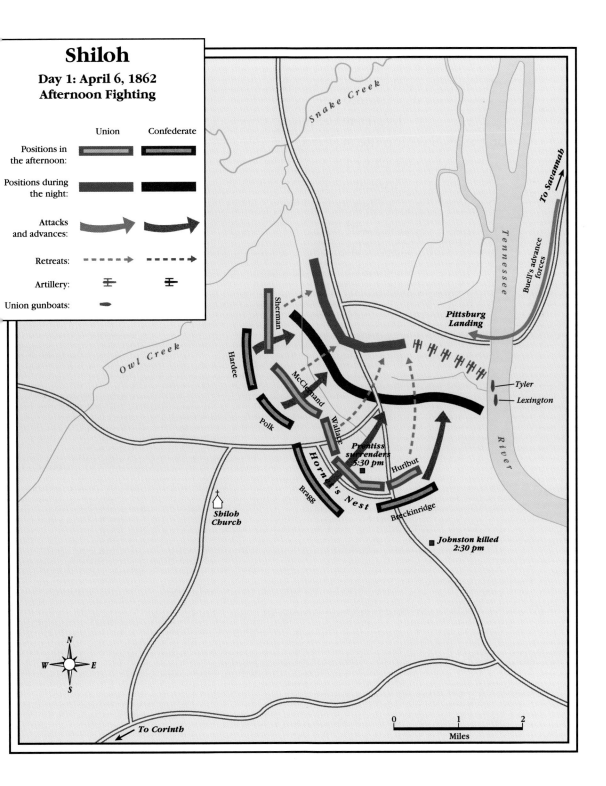

Shiloh

Day 1: April 6, 1862
Afternoon Fighting

	Union	Confederate
Positions in the afternoon:		
Positions during the night:		
Attacks and advances:		
Retreats:		
Artillery:		
Union gunboats:		

Snake Creek

Tennessee

To Savannab

Buell's advance forces

Pittsburg Landing

Owl Creek

Sherman

Hardee

McClernand

Wallace

Tyler

Lexington

Polk

River

Prentiss surrenders 5:30 pm

Hornet's Nest

Hurlbut

Bragg

Breckinridge

Shiloh Church

Johnston killed 2:30 pm

N
W—E
S

To Corinth

0   1   2
Miles

< 38 >

As his boot gradually filled with blood, however, Johnston grew weaker and was removed from his horse—the bullet had cut a large blood vessel. Johnston's aides gathered around their commander. They attempted to revive him, but there was little they could do. By 2:30 P.M. Johnston had bled to death.

This all happened suddenly. At first the troops were not told of Johnston's death for fear that they would be too upset to continue fighting. Beauregard, who succeeded Johnston as commander, immediately ordered a massive artillery attack on the Union line in the Hornet's Nest and in the orchard. With more than 50 big guns being fired, and men dying on all sides, the Union soldiers finally surrendered to the Confederates at 5:30 P.M. They had held back the Confederate advance for more than six crucial hours. As evening came, and it became difficult to see, the fighting died down. Beauregard wired President Jefferson Davis that his army had defeated Grant's forces.

Night of Horror

The night brought new horrors. As darkness fell, the bodies of hundreds of dead and wounded soldiers still lay on the battlefield. A storm arose, and in the flashes of lightning, surviving soldiers could see wild hogs feeding on the dead bodies. Throughout that terrible night, the moans and screams of the wounded men pierced the darkness. Many of the victims cried for water. Soon the skies opened up and torrential rain fell on the battlefield. The next morning, Sergeant Ambrose G. Bierce of the 9th Indiana Regiment saw that gunfire had ignited the underbrush, and many of the wounded men had burned to death. He wrote that "at every point...lay the bodies, half buried in the ashes; some in the unlovely looseness of attitude denoting sudden death by a bullet, but by far the greater number in postures of agony that told of the tormenting flame."[8]

Although second in command at Shiloh on the first day of battle, P. G. T. Beauregard was in many ways more popular at the time than his commander, Albert Sidney Johnston. Beauregard had been in charge of the Confederate forces that attacked Fort Sumter in April 1861. Later that year, in July, he was second in command at the battle of Bull Run, Virginia—a major Confederate victory in the Civil War.

Pierre Gustave Toutant Beauregard

Beauregard was born in St. Bernard Parish, Louisiana, in 1818. He graduated from West Point in 1838 and began his career as an engineer in the U.S. Army. Beauregard served under General Winfield Scott during the Mexican War in 1847, and he played a major role in the conquest of Mexico City.

In January 1861, Beauregard was appointed the head of cadets at West Point. He held this post for only five days, however, resigning from the U.S. Army at the start of the war in loyalty to the South. Shortly thereafter, Beauregard was appointed Confederate brigadier-general and given command of Charleston, South Carolina.

After Fort Sumter, Beauregard served in northern Virginia. Following the battle of Bull Run, he was reassigned to the West as second in command of Johnston's army. When Johnston was killed in the battle of Shiloh on April 6, 1862, Beauregard assumed command of the army. On the second day of battle, he saw his forces pushed back and began the retreat to Corinth, Mississippi.

Shortly after Shiloh, a combination of ill health and friction with President Davis led to Beauregard's removal from command. Davis, however, brought him back in 1862, and made him commander of the Georgia and South Carolina coastal region. Beauregard spent the final weeks of the war fighting alongside the Confederate general J. E. Johnston in North Carolina.

After General Robert E. Lee's surrender in 1865, Beauregard returned to Louisiana and went into business. He became president of a railroad and even served for a time as head of the Louisiana state lottery. Highly regarded in his day as a brilliant engineer, Beauregard died in 1893 at the age of 75.

< 40 >

A Confederate nurse later wrote that "Nothing that I have ever heard or read had given me the faintest idea of the horrors witnessed there."[9]

So awful were the sounds of suffering that Grant abandoned his headquarters and slept under a tree far enough away from the dying men so that he couldn't hear their cries. But Grant had not given up. No matter how severe the casualties, he would always be ready to fight again. "Lick 'em tomorrow," Grant said to one of his commanders.[10]

Beauregard's telegram to Jefferson Davis had been premature. One of Johnston's goals had been to block a Union retreat to the river. Pittsburg Landing, however, remained in Union hands. All through the night, Union gunboats fired randomly into the Confederate camp. The soldiers who were not killed spent a terror-filled, sleepless night listening to the whine of the incoming shells.

This drawing shows the Union gunboats at Pittsburg Landing on the evening of the first day of battle.

When the Civil War broke out in 1861, President Abraham Lincoln called for volunteers to aid the Union cause. In the early days of the war, there was no draft—the calling up of young men into the military—as there would be later in the war and in future wars fought by the United States.

Instead, each state sent units to fight for the national government. The units were made up of young men who offered their services for a year in return for pay.

In almost all states, the minimum age for volunteers was 18. Many younger boys were eager to serve, however, and recruiters sometimes looked the other way when a boy younger than 18 wanted to enlist. Many young men of 16 or 17 thus found themselves fighting in the war. The youngest enlistees, however, were frequently used as drummer boys. They were responsible for playing the drums before and during a battle. Although the drummer boys were also supposed to be at least 18 years old, sometimes they were as young as 9 or 10.

Many sources report that one of the drummer boys at Shiloh was 10-year-old John Clem, a volunteer with the 21st Michigan Regiment who had run away from home to join the army. During the battle, an artillery shell had smashed his drum, but left young John unhurt. He soon became famous as "Johnny Shiloh, the Drummer Boy of Shiloh." (Some historians now report that John Clem was not actually at Shiloh.)

In 1863, he received more fame at the battle of Chickamauga in Georgia. At this battle, the Confederates inflicted serious losses on the Union forces. As the Union army was retreating, John Clem was riding on top of a caisson—a wagon carrying artillery ammunition. Suddenly, a Confederate soldier appeared and attempted to steal the caisson. The 11-year-old John shot the soldier and by doing so prevented the Union army's ammunition from falling into Confederate hands.

John Clem's Civil War service was the beginning of a long and distinguished career in the army. When he retired as a major-general, in 1915, during World War I, he had served more than 50 years—his entire adult life—in the military.

< 42 >

Under cover of darkness, Buell's forces began arriving to rein-
force Grant's battered army. By boat and on foot, 25,000 fresh troops
slipped into camp; the first ones to arrive took up positions on the
bluffs of Pittsburg Landing. Grant's prayers had been answered.
His army had been replenished—and he intended to take action as
soon as the sun came up.

The Battle: Day Two, April 7, 1862

At dawn, Grant unleashed his army against the bleary-eyed
Confederate soldiers. The Southerners fought back furiously despite
their exhaustion. The newly strengthened Union forces, however,
were too powerful. The fighting raged on for hours as the Union
army inched forward. The fields and forest were once again covered
with dead bodies and with wounded men screaming for help. A hor-
rified Confederate soldier, George Asbury Bruton of the 19th
Louisiana Regiment, wrote in a letter two days later that "never did
I think it would be my lot to participate in such a horrible scene. . . .
I never want to witness any such scene. It seems as if I can hear the
groans of the dying & wounded men and the cannons roaring all the
time worse than any thunderstorms that ever was heard."[11]

By 2:00 in the afternoon of April 7, the Confederate units had
been pushed back as far as Shiloh Church. They had lost all the
ground won the previous day. As the Union forces continued to
advance, Beauregard realized that he had no choice but to order a
retreat. The Confederates streamed back toward Corinth, Mississippi.

Most of the Union leaders ordered their men not to pursue the
retreating Southerners. For a time, however, General Sherman sent
his units to follow and attack the fleeing Confederates. At one point,
Confederate cavalry troops about four miles southwest of Shiloh
Church, under Colonel Nathan Bedford Forrest, turned and charged

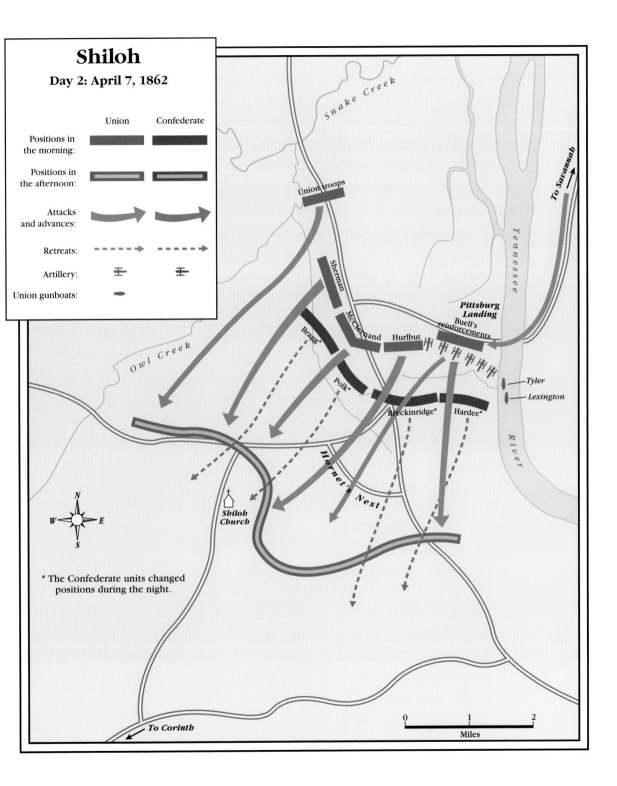

Shiloh

Day 2: April 7, 1862

	Union	Confederate
Positions in the morning:		
Positions in the afternoon:		
Attacks and advances:		
Retreats:		
Artillery:		
Union gunboats:		

Union troops

Snake Creek

To Savannah

Sherman

McClernand

Bragg*

Hurlbut

Pittsburg Landing
Buell's reinforcements

Polk*

Tyler

Lexington

Breckinridge*

Hardee*

Owl Creek

Tennessee River

Hornet's Nest

Shiloh Church

N
W E
S

* The Confederate units changed positions during the night.

To Corinth

0	1	2
Miles

< 44 >

headlong into Sherman's forces. Forrest, a colorful and fearless man, led the charge. But as he galloped ahead, wildly swinging his saber, he discovered that his men had not followed him. Caught directly in the midst of the Union forces, Forrest was wounded and decided to end the attack.

When the shooting finally stopped, the Shiloh battlefield was a nightmarish scene. Grant later said that there were so many corpses on the ground that it would have been possible to "walk across the clearing…stepping on dead bodies without a foot touching the ground."[12] Mass graves were hastily dug. "When the grave was ready," one soldier recalled, "we placed the bodies therein, two deep. All the monument reared to those brave men was a board upon which I cut with my pocket knife the words '125 rebels.' We buried our Union boys in a separate trench and on another board cut '35 Union.' "[13]

The Loss of the West

Nearly 110,000 men fought in the battle of Shiloh. Almost 3,500 died and another 16,000 were wounded during the two days of fighting. There were almost as many casualties at Shiloh as in the entire American Revolution. At that point in the Civil War, Shiloh was the bloodiest battle to date.

Technically, the battle was a tie. The Union did not win a clear victory, nor were the Confederates overwhelmingly defeated. For the next few weeks, the Union army moved slowly toward Corinth. General Halleck demoted Grant and was convinced that the Confederates would launch a counterattack at any moment. Halleck hoped that Beauregard would simply leave Corinth without a fight.

Grant was disgusted by the Union's lack of speed and agression. Although he wanted to pursue the Confederate army and

For the soldiers who survived Shiloh the battle would never be forgotten. Some wrote home to relatives shortly after the battle. Others wrote about their experiences years later. Many of the eyewitness accounts have survived and give us a close-up look at this terrible event.

T. Lyle Dickey, a Union soldier, wrote a letter to his aunt a few days after the battle. He describes his regiment's pursuit of Confederate troops on April 7:

My regiment was first on the ground & in thirty minutes we had at our heels 2,000 cavalry. Just then it was discovered the enemy was bringing cannon in…battery a 1/4 of a mile & in thick brush unapproachable by charge of cavalry. Gen'l Grant ordered us to halt & wait for orders & he road to our left. Seeing this mass of cavalry, I thought we would be merely a target for the shells of the enemy and moved my regiment to the left to a ravine, near by & ordered the rest to the right & left.[14]

A Tennessee private described the horror of the battle scene to his relatives back home:

Men…lying in every conceivable position; the dead…with their eyes wide open, the wounded begging piteously for help.… I seemed in a sort of daze.[15]

General William Tecumseh Sherman summed up his reaction in a letter:

The scene on this field would have cured anybody of war.[16]

In one intance, a Union captain actually had the chance to speak with a wounded Confederate soldier on the battlefield. As he approached the dying man, the Union captain noticed that,

He was covered with clotted blood, pillowing his head on the dead body of a comrade. The first thing he said to me was 'Oh God! What made you come down here to fight us? We never would have come up there.'[17]

Soldiers on both sides realized they had been in a tremendous battle. Although no one then could have known the outcome of the war, they were all deeply affected by their experiences at the battle of Shiloh.

The losses at Shiloh were great—it was the Civil War's bloodiest battle to date.

attack, Grant had been overruled. In Washington, Halleck's allies were once again denouncing Grant to President Lincoln, calling him reckless and a drunk. Lincoln, however, knew better. "Drunk or not," he said, "I can't spare this man. He fights!"[18]

< 47 >

When the Union army finally entered Corinth, the Confederates had already moved further south to Tupelo, Mississippi. They had left behind a ghost town where, as one Union officer wrote, the Northerners found "not a bite of bacon."[19]

In the long run, Shiloh turned out to be a devastating loss for the Confederacy. The battle weakened the Confederate forces in the region, and they never fully recovered. In addition, when the Union forces finally arrived in Corinth, they took control of the rail line to Memphis and were able to start applying pressure to that vital city on the Mississippi.

Shiloh, in fact, was the first step toward realization of one of the Union's major goals in the West: control of the Mississippi River. Within two months, the Confederates would surrender Memphis, and New Orleans would be occupied by the Union army. In 1863, Grant enjoyed one of his most brilliant victories—the capture of the strategic river town of Vicksburg, Mississippi. With the Mississippi River under Union control, the Confederacy was now divided. Shiloh was the beginning of the Confederate loss of the West.

HISTORY REMEMBERED

The Civil War ended in April 1865, when the Southern commander, General Robert E. Lee, surrendered his army to the head of the Union forces, General Ulysses S. Grant, at Appomattox, Virginia.

The war had left more than 625,000 dead. In the 1860s, it was not possible to return the bodies of those men who had fallen in battle to their loved ones hundreds of miles away.

Instead, they were placed in hastily created cemeteries on the actual sites of the great battles. In places such as Gettysburg in Pennsylvania, Antietam in Maryland, Vicksburg in Mississippi, Shiloh in Tennessee, and in countless others, thousands of soldiers who were killed were buried side by side.

In the years after the war, many of these battle sites were designated national memorials by Congress in order to honor both the Union and Confederate dead. Visitors could then visit the actual battlefields and pay their respects to the brave soldiers who fought on both sides of the conflict.

Shiloh National Military Park

The battlefield at Shiloh was officially preserved as the Shiloh National Military Park by an act of Congress in 1894. The park contains 3,962 acres and has within its boundaries the Shiloh National Cemetery as well as preserved prehistoric Indian mounds that are listed as historic landmarks.

Visitors can pay their respects to those who died at Shiloh by visiting the cemetery or the five mass graves of Confederate soldiers on the battlefield. They may also tour the battlefield site and visit a

< 49 >

The grounds of the Shiloh National Military Park include more than 95 percent of the historic battlefield.

museum that contains original rifles, pistols, muskets, cannons and bullets recovered from the battlefield. "Living History" demonstrations are held several times each year.

Location and Address Shiloh National Military Park, Route 1, Box 9, Shiloh, TN 38376. Telephone: (901) 689-5696 (Visitor Center); (901) 689-3475 (bookstore).

Operating Hours Daily, 8:00 A.M.–5:00 P.M., all year. It is closed December 25. The busiest season is from April through Labor Day, especially on weekends during the summer.

< 51 >

Entrance Fees $2 per person; $4 per family. Group rates are also available. There is no fee for scouts or educational groups.

Exhibits The museum has exhibits that display items from the battlefield, including tin cups, pots, and dishes used by Union and Confederate forces. Other pieces of equipment, such as knapsacks, cartridge boxes, belts, and artillery shells are also on display. An orientation film is shown at the Visitor Center. Park officials recommend that visitors view the film first before exploring the grounds.

Soldiers who died in the battle of Shiloh are honored with these markers at Shiloh National Cemetery.

< 52 >

Programs and Special Events Visitors may explore the park on their own or may join one of the park ranger guided tours (which vary in length) that are available from Memorial Day through Labor Day. "Living History" demonstrations are held on weekends nearest the date (April 6–7) of the battle. These demonstrations include the firing of Civil War weapons.

A large collection of authentic artillery pieces is assembled for these demonstrations. Volunteers dressed as soldiers of the period help to bring the memorable battle to life for modern audiences. Commemorative ceremonies are also held each year in May, on Memorial Day.

Using the Park Shiloh National Military Park is wheelchair accessible in all areas. There are restaurants, convenience stores, and grocery stores available nearby. There is also a bookstore on the premises. Motor vehicles and bicycles are allowed in the park. Recreational vehicles and buses may be left in the parking lots or can travel on certain roads.

Related Points of Interest

Corinth, Mississippi

There are several points of interest relating to Shiloh in the vicinity of the park. At Corinth, Mississippi, is the Corinth National Cemetery. It contains the remains of Union soldiers who died during the Civil War campaign around Corinth.

An annual reenactment of a Civil War battle that took place at Corinth is held each October. The sounds of cannon fire can be heard some four miles away in the town itself, much like the sounds that the townspeople heard in 1862.

Also in Corinth is the Northeast Mississippi Museum. It contains many exhibits relating to the Civil War in northern Mississippi.

< 53 >

Location and Address Northeast Mississippi Museum, corner of Washington and Fourth streets, Corinth, Mississippi 38834. Telephone: (601) 287-3120.

Operating Hours 10:00 A.M.–5:00 P.M. Monday to Saturday, and 2:00 P.M.–5:00 P.M. Sunday. It is closed on all national and religious holidays.

Entrance Fees Admission is free.

Exhibits The museum has displays relating to Corinth history as well as files of letters and diaries written by Civil War soldiers while they were in Corinth. Artifacts from other Civil War battles are also exhibited here.

Vicksburg National Military Park

Vicksburg National Military Park is located on the Mississippi River. It was established in 1899 to commemorate the campaign, siege, and defense of Vicksburg, Mississippi, which took place between March and July 1863.

The Vicksburg battlefield has been preserved, with more than 1,300 monuments and markers, reconstructed trenches, 125 cannons, and a restored Union gunboat. The *USS Cairo*, a 175-foot boat sunk by the Confederates in December 1862, was raised from the bottom of the Yazoo River and restored in 1964. The park also contains the *Cairo* Museum and the Vicksburg National Cemetery. The cemetery is the site of 18,000 graves of American soldiers—graves dating from the Civil War through World War II.

Location and Address Vicksburg National Military Park, 3201 Clay Street, Vicksburg, Mississippi 39180. Telephone: (601) 636-0583 (Visitor Center); (601) 636-2199 (*Cairo* Museum).

Operating Hours Daily, 8:00 A.M.–5:00 P.M. (Visitor Center); *Cairo* Museum, 8:30 A.M.–5:00 P.M. (November–March), 9:30 A.M.–6:00 P.M. (April–October). The park is closed December 25.

< 54 >

Entrance Fees Daily admission is $4.00 per vehicle and $2.00 per noncommercial bus passenger. Special annual passes are available for groups and for senior citizens.

Exhibits The *Cairo* Museum houses many personal and military items such as clothing, cups, plates, utensils, and weaponry found on the *Cairo* when it was salvaged. The partially restored gunboat itself, which rests near the museum, has its original pilot house, cannons, engines, and boilers.

The Visitor Center, at the Clay Street entrance, offers public information, a bookstore, rest rooms, and telephones. Facilities in the park are wheelchair accessible.

Programs and Events A 16-mile tour road runs parallel to the Union and Confederate siege lines. The road passes a number of historic spots. Various short trails to points of interest start off from this road. Guided tours of the park are available on request and reservations are preferred. Costs for guided tours are $20 per car, $30 per van, and $40 per bus. Call (601) 636-3827 for information.

A narrated, self-guided driving tour is available on cassette tape. It can be rented or purchased at the Visitor Center.

Fort Donelson National Battlefield

Located in Tennessee, this is the site of Grant's first major victory over the Confederate army. The 536-acre site includes Fort Donelson National Cemetery, the Dover Hotel (where the Confederates surrendered to Grant), and Fort Donelson. The cemetery was established in 1867 and the park was designated a national battlefield in 1928.

Location and Address Fort Donelson National Battlefield, P.O. Box 434, Dover, TN 37058-0434. Telephone: (615) 232-5348.

Operating Hours Daily, 8:00 A.M.–5:00 P.M. (Visitor Center); Dover Hotel, 12:00 P.M.–4:00 P.M. (June–September). The hotel is closed from October to May. The entire park is closed December 25.

The Fort Donelson National Battlefield preserves the site of Grant's first major victory over Confederate troops.

Entrance Fees Admission is free, and donations are accepted at the Visitor Center.

Exhibits The Dover Hotel is a historic restoration of the building where Confederate General Simon Buckner surrendered to General Grant in 1862.

The remains of Fort Donelson contain earthen fortifications (walls and trenches made of dirt) and cannons. Visitors are not

< 56 >

allowed to climb or walk on any of the historic remains within the battlefield. Visitors are also prohibited from digging in the ground for battlefield momentos that may still be buried there. The Visitor Center and the Dover Hotel are both wheelchair accessible.

Programs and Special Events During the summer months, special demonstrations of period costumes and historical events associated with Fort Donelson are held for the benefit of visitors. These are not presented on any regular schedule—call ahead for information.

Visitors may explore the site on the five miles of trails that are used for hiking. The park may also be toured by car, and cassette tours are available.

Guided tours can also be arranged upon request for groups only and require reservations at least four weeks in advance.

General Grant National Memorial

After his death in 1885, Grant was buried in a temporary tomb in Riverside Park in New York City. Plans were begun almost immediately for an elaborate permanent tomb in the park. Commonly referred to as "Grant's Tomb," the huge stone mausoleum rests on three-quarters of an acre of land overlooking the Hudson River.

The memorial was dedicated in 1897, and was designated a national memorial in 1958. It contains the coffins of Grant and his wife, as well as a small museum.

Location and Address General Grant National Memorial, 122nd Street and Riverside Drive, New York, New York 10027. Telephone: (212) 666-1640.

Operating Hours Daily, 9:00 A.M.–5:00 P.M. The memorial is closed Christmas Day.

Entrance Fees Admission is free.

< 57 >

Exhibits   The museum on the main floor contains murals depicting events in Grant's life as well as photographs, reproductions of newspapers, and maps from various times in his life.

In a recessed area below the main floor are the two coffins. Visitors may take the marble staircase down to the lower level and view the coffins and the statues of famous Civil War generals that surround them.

Because of the stairs leading to the main entrance, the memorial is not wheelchair accessible. Although there are no guided tours, museum guards are available to answer questions.

Special Events   The memorial underwent extensive cleaning and restoration in preparation for its 100th anniversary celebration in 1997.

The stately General Grant National Memorial is located in New York City.

All of these sites have been preserved so that people can continue to learn about the Civil War and can pay tribute to all the Americans who lost their lives in that conflict.

CHRONOLOGY OF THE CIVIL WAR

November 1860	Abraham Lincoln, Republican, elected president of the United States.
December 1860	South Carolina becomes the first Southern state to secede from the Union.
March 4, 1861	Lincoln sworn in as president.
February 1861	Six Southern states that had seceded form the Confederate States of America.
April 1861	Confederate forces fire on Union Fort Sumter in Charleston, SC, and the Civil War begins.
July 1861	Union forces defeated at the battle of Bull Run in Virginia. First major battle of the war.
February 1862	Forts Henry and Donelson, in Kentucky, captured by Union forces under General Ulysses S. Grant.
April 1862	Battle of Shiloh
September 1862	Union soldiers push back Confederate invasion of Maryland at the battle of Antietam.
December 1862	Union suffers massive casualties at the battle of Fredericksburg, in Virginia.
January 1863	Lincoln issues the Emancipation Proclamation, freeing all slaves in Confederate territories.
May 1863	Confederates decisively defeat Union forces at the battle of Chancellorsville, Virginia.
July 1863	Grant's army captures Vicksburg, Mississippi, completing the Union takeover of the Mississippi River, splitting the Confederacy in two.
	Union forces under General George Meade push back the invading Confederate army under

< 59 >

	General Robert E. Lee at the Battle of Gettysburg, Pennsylvania.
	The last Confederate attempt to invade the North.
March 1864	General Grant appointed head of all Union forces by President Lincoln.
May–July 1864	Grant's army marches into Virginia and begins a series of bloody battles with Lee's forces across the state from north to south.
August 1864– April 1865	Grant and Lee dig in for a long siege of trench warfare south of Petersburg, Virginia. The siege will last 9 months.
September 1864	General William Tecumseh Sherman captures Atlanta, Georgia. Sherman begins his famous "March to the Sea."
late 1864	Sherman marches through Georgia, burning everything in his path, and reaches Savannah on Christmas Day.
January 1865	Sherman turns north and marches into South Carolina, burning the capital, Columbia, to the ground.
March 1865	Grant breaks through at Petersburg and chases Lee's army into Virginia.
April 1865	Richmond, capital of the Confederacy, falls to Union forces. Lincoln enters the Confederate headquarters and sits in Jefferson Davis's chair.
April 1865	Lee surrenders to Grant at Appomattox. Lincoln is assassinated a few days later.
May 1865	End of hostilities with the surrender of General E. Kirby Smith at Shreveport, Louisiana.
April 1866	President Andrew Johnson declares the Civil War officially over.

FURTHER READING

Colman, Penny. *Spies! Women in the Civil War*. Cincinnati, OH: Betterway Books, 1992.

Dudley, William, and John C. Chalberg, eds. *The Civil War: Opposing Viewpoints*. San Diego, CA: Greenhaven Press, 1995.

Hakim, Joy. *War, Terrible War*. New York: Oxford University Press, History of US, Book Six, 1994.

Kent, Zachary. *The Civil War: "A House Divided."* Hillsdale, NJ: Enslow, 1992.

Marrin, Albert. *Unconditional Surrender: U.S. Grant and the Civil War*. New York: Atheneum, 1994.

Ray, Delia. *Behind the Blue & Gray: The Soldier's Life in the Civil War*. New York: Dutton Children's Books, 1991.

Reef, Catherine. *Civil War Soldiers* (African-American Soldiers Series). New York: Twenty-First Century Books, 1993.

Smith, Carter, ed. *The First Battles: A Sourcebook on the Civil War*. Brookfield, CT: Millbrook Press, 1993.

Steins, Richard. *The Nation Divides: The Civil War (1820-1880)*. New York: Twenty-First Century Books, 1993.

WEB SITES

There are thousands of sites on the World Wide Web related to the Civil War. One way to explore them is to go to a site called "Civil War Related Web Links Index." This site is an index of places to go to for a variety of information. It will tell you where to find accounts of battles, photographs, maps, music, and much more. The Web address is:

http://www.cwc.1su.edu/civlink.htm

< 61 >

A Web page that deals exclusively with the battle of Shiloh is found at:

http://www.itek.net/~gpg/

Here you will find historic maps, personal accounts of the battle, and photographs.

For useful information about Shiloh National Military Park you may go directly to the park's Web page at:

http://www.nps.gov.shil

For an in-depth look at the history of the Tennessee-Mississippi region where the battle of Shiloh occurred, go to the following Web page:

http://www2.tsixroads.com/Corinth_MLSANDY/corhis.html

This page will lead you to rich resources, including photographs, diaries and letters of Union and Confederate troops, written histories, timelines, and additional sites to explore.

If you are interested in Civil War songs and poems, you may find a large number at the following Web site:

http://www.gulf.net/~vbraun.FlaStar/songs.html

American Memory is a Library of Congress website that features American history:

http://memory.loc.gov

http://lcweb2.loc.gov/am mem/ndlpedu

SOURCE NOTES

Part One

1. James Thomas Flexner, *Washington: The Indispensable Man* (Boston: Little, Brown, 1969), p. 328.

2. Quoted in Allen C. Guelzo, *The Crisis of the American Republic: A History of the Civil War and Reconstruction* (New York: St. Martin's Press, 1995), p. 78.

< **62** >

3. *Abraham Lincoln: Speeches and Writings, 1859–1865* (New York: Library of America, 1989), pp. 223, 224.

Part Two

1. Quoted in Geoffrey C. Ward, Ric Burns, and Ken Burns, *The Civil War: An Illustrated History* (New York: Knopf, 1990), p. 98.

2. Ulysses S. Grant, "The Battle of Shiloh," in *Battles and Leaders of the Civil War*, vol.2, eds. C. C. Buel and R. U. Johnson (New York: Macmillan, 1956), pp. 485–486.

3. Quoted in Guelzo, *The Crisis of the American Republic*, p. 349.

4. William T. Sherman, *The Memoirs of General W. T. Sherman* (New York: The Library of America, 1990), p. 627.

5. Ward, Burns, and Burns, *The Civil War*, p. 113.

6. Ibid.

7. Curt Johnson and Mark McLaughlin, *Battles of the Civil War: From Bull Run to Petersburg—Four Years of Hard Strategy and Bloodshed* (New York: Roxby Press, 1977), p. 45.

8. Quoted in Allen C. Guelzo, *The Crisis of the American Republic*, p. 156.

9. Quoted in Ward, Burns, and Burns, *The Civil War*, p. 113.

10. Ibid., p. 121

11. Quoted in Bruce Catton, *Grant Moves South* (Boston: Little, Brown, 1960), p. 242.

12. Quoted in Ward, Burns, and Burns, *The Civil War*, p. 121.

13. Ibid.

14. Letter of T. Lyle Dickey (no date). Text of full letter may be found on the Internet at: **http://www.itek.net/~gpg/**

15. Quoted in James M. McPherson, *The Battle Cry of Freedom: The Civil War Era* (New York: Oxford University Press, 1988), p. 413.

16. Ibid.

< 63 >

17. Ward, Burns, and Burns, *The Civil War*, p. 121.

18. Quoted in Johnson and McLaughlin, *Battles of the Civil War*, p. 46.

19. Ibid., p. 50.

OTHER SOURCES

Henretta, James, W., W. Elliot Brownlee, David Brody, and Susan Ware, *America's History,* 2nd edition. New York: Worth, 1993.

Kunhardt, Philip B., Jr., Philip B. Kunhardt III, and Peter W. Kunhardt, *Lincoln: An Illustrated Biography.* New York: Knopf, 1992.

Thomas, Emory M., *The Confederate Nation: 1861-1865.* New York: Harper & Row, 1979.

Wiley, Bell Irvin, *The Life of Billy Yank: The Common Soldier of the Union.* Baton Rouge, LA.: LSU Press, 1984.

_____. *The Life of Johnny Reb: The Common Soldier of the Confederacy.* Baton Rouge, LA: LSU Press, 1984.

INDEX